The Magic of the Blessed Mother's Miracles

Mary Salerno Meehan
Swami Sadashiva Tirtha

 Peaceful Press

PeacefulPress.com

ISBN: 9798850634612

©Copyright 2023 Mary Salerno Meehan and Swami Sadashiva Tirtha.
All rights reserved.

Disclaimer: This book is for education and entertainment purposes only. It is not intended to treat, diagnose, heal, or cure any psychological condition.

No portion of this book may be reproduced in any form or by any means, electronic or mechanical, including photocopying, recording, or by any information storage and refried system without written permission, except for short quotes used in reviews, articles, or multimedia.

Dedication

There's stories and then there's stories. The ones with any worth change your life forever, perhaps only in a small way, but once you've heard them, they are forever a part of you.

You nurture them and pass them on, and the giving only makes you feel better. The others are just words on a page.

Charles de Lint

To my husband Jimmy, who served 20 years on the NY Police Department as a Police Officer, Detective and Sergeant, and was a first responder on 9-11. We've shared our lives together since our first date, the night before Thanksgiving 1980. He is my hero.

To my parents from whom I learned about generosity of heart and the love of Blessed Mother. Thank you Blessed Mother for giving them 64 magical years together.

To all those who are aspiring to put their whole heart and soul into a relationship with spirit, God, Blessed Mother, whatever it may be, and changing your life forever.

Introduction

I believe my spiritual signs & validations began with forgiveness

Mary Salerno Meehan

In the early 80's I felt called to start attending weekly Novenas and hosting a weekly Rosary at my home.

I notice I felt such a connection with the Blessed Mother. Following her advice, I prayed from my heart, and instantly I saw each prayer being answered.

She wasn't just a figure in the sky or in heaven; she was so real and pure and full of love. It overwhelmed me.

I thought, *It's not fair to keep this to myself. I need to share it with others. I'm just an ordinary human being. If she could help me she could help anyone. All it takes is praying from the heart and soul — with your own being.*

Blessed Mother I want to write a book and share with the world all the blessings that you bestowed upon me, and how you are continually blessing me with the grace of peace. In this way they too may know what you can do for them.

Know that of all devotions, the most pleasing to Mary is to have frequent recourse to her, asking for favors.
St. Alphonsus Liguori

Table of Contents

Dedication..........................ii
Introduction.......................v

Part 1: Miracle Stories

What is the Meaning of Life?....1
My Journey Begins................6
A Rose by Any Other Name....20
Praying from My Heart..........26
Rita's Story........................32
The Bracelet.......................40
Guess Whose Coming
to Dinner?..........................47
When Johnny Comes
Marching Home...................63
Relative Miracles.................72
    Nana Salerno................74
    Mama Mia.....................80
    Maria Spina Caligiuri.........85
    Blue Jay Way.................92

Pop Goes the Cardinal.....95
Daughter Knows Best......97
Touched By An Angel.....103
Anna from Grace................110
Conchita Who?...................115
Saved By An Angel.............126
Life After Life.....................133
Rainbows and Rain............141
Summary..........................148

Part 2:
Finding Peace Through Grace

<u>Receiving Signs</u>
Lessons I Learned..............149
Penny for Your Thoughts......151
Another Penny for
Your Thoughts...................157
Beautiful Boy....................164
Traces of Love..................169
Tools I Use......................173
Summary.................. 197
Epilogue.........................200

Spread love everywhere you go. Let no one ever come to you without leaving happier.

Saint Teresa of Calcutta
(Mother Teresa)

What is the Meaning of Life?

My life was a constant whirlwind; always on the go. I commuted to Wall Street on weekdays and to my second job working for a psychologist, Thursday nights and Saturdays.

At the same time I was renovating my house on Staten Island; taking down walls—there wasn't a full wall left when I was done, and the clean-up was physically demanding. It reminded me of the Mel Brooks movie, *High Anxiety*. With all these things going on, do you think I slowed down? No, I decided to have a baby too.

To my surprise, expecting a baby made my life even better. I was very happy. Then about 4 months in I started getting abdominal pains. The doctor looked at the sonogram and said you have a 50-50 chance of a miscarriage and put me on full bed rest. So much for less stress.

I was very worried about losing the baby. I saw the concern in Jimmy's eyes and I felt saddened. I followed the doctor's advice and stayed in bed for almost a month. During that time I said the Rosary twice a day and prayed to the Blessed Mother to surround this baby with the Holy Spirit and keep it safe. After weeks of prayers, I started feeling better. I was so grateful.

In 1988, my prayers were answered. James Meehan Jr. was born happy and healthy. My first child. He was so sweet and gentle. The Blessed Mother answered my prayers and protected my baby. This was the first of many answered prayers to come.

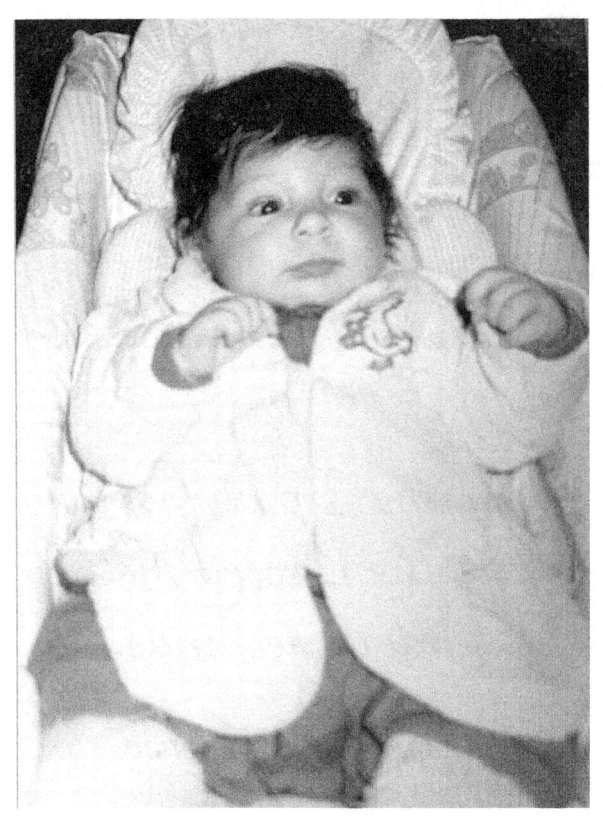

Sweet Baby James

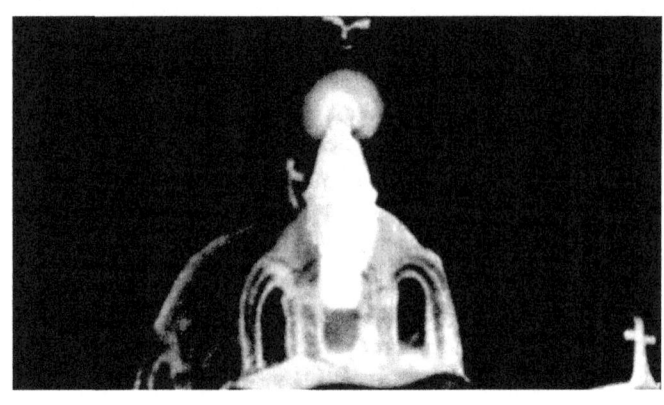

Every time I pray from my heart, the Blessed Mother tenderly responds.

Mary Salerno Meehan

The Journey Begins

Never could I have imagined that this ordinary day can turn into something so extraordinary. It was a warm sunny day and I was heading to work on Wall Street. I got on my morning bus and sat in my usual seat.

That's when I noticed this eloquently dressed woman sitting behind me holding a smaller version of the Rosary. The beads were iridescent lavender; it was breathtaking. I had to ask her where she got them. She graciously replied that she got them from the church and they are called Saint Theresa beads.

Although I heard of Saint Theresa, I wasn't too familiar with her story. The woman said that Saint Theresa showers us with roses and that she is a very beloved, powerful saint. I asked her what her name was and she replied Marie. I said my name was Mary and it was so nice to meet her.

Marie said that she went to the Miraculous Medal Novena on Monday nights, and invited me to join her. I was so excited, I said of course. This is how my journey began.

Why did I agree to go to church tonight? I wondered. I had a very busy life. I work till 7:30 at night. They would be picking me up at 7:45. All I wanted to do is eat, watch TV, shower, and go to bed. What in God's name made me agree to this? I was just about to call and tell them I couldn't go when they beeped the horn.

Marie and her three friends, Anna, Theresa, and Kitty, picked me up. *I hope I don't fall asleep on the way*, I thought. Exhausted, I stepped into the chapel. But then, suddenly, I was revived.

It felt like I was in an old-world stone grotto, warmly embracing me. The smell of the incense was so entrancing. The room was darkened with flickering candles that emanated such a peaceful atmosphere. I sat in front of a beautiful statue of the Blessed Mother holding the baby Jesus.

I immediately said to myself, *Wow, I love this!* I was so glad I came. I felt like a little kid again, praying in St. Adalbert's grotto at my grammar school. After a crazy day on Wall Street, it doesn't get better than this. No need for Grandpa's wine tonight.

St. Adalbert's Grotto

As we said the Novena, I heard the phrase, "Ever while wearing this Miraculous Medal, may we be blessed by your loving protection." I noticed that everyone there was wearing a Miraculous Medal and I really wanted one too.

On our way home I asked the girls how can I get a miraculous medal. I was excited and anxious to have one. "Where can I get that medal, where can I find one?" I pestered them all the way home. I remember it like it was yesterday.

When I got home, I began folding the laundry, still wondering how I can get that medal. As I was putting away my husband Jimmy's bloomers, I was shocked to see a Miraculous Medal sitting on the bottom of his drawer. I got so excited that I immediately called Jimmy at work.

I screamed, "Jimmy where did you get that medal in your draw?"

Jimmy replied, "I found it on the street, picked it up, and brought it home. If you want it, it's yours."

I said, "Jimmy I just told the Blessed Mother an hour ago that I really want to have a Miraculous Medal and here it is in your bloomer drawer."

The Miraculous Medal

I was thrilled as I hung up the phone. *How could this have happened?*, I thought. I wanted this medal so badly and there it was waiting for me.

During that week, I saw Marie on the bus, and I told her how I found the medal. I was so excited my prayers were answered within just two hours. Marie said, "You are so blessed to have your prayers answered immediately." And to think it was sitting there waiting for me — that gave me chills.

It was no surprise that I was sitting in this peaceful chapel the following week again. Of course, I was wearing the Miraculous Medal around my neck.

While praying the Novena, I was staring at the Blessed Mother's statue in front of me. I had so much faith, and I knew she was with me. I felt true love from her. I knelt down, looked at her, and felt that love connection as easy as turning on a light switch.

After reciting the Novena I realized I was in deep prayer, crying tears of joy. Later, on our drive home, I told the girls that this Novena was so beautiful that I wanted to hold a Rosary at my home once a week. They immediately agreed.

We were so excited about doing this. We had so many people that needed our prayers. To us, the Rosary was special and powerful. This was praying directly to the Blessed Mother while meditating on the mysteries of her son.

So began our weekly gatherings at my home for the Rosary,

talking about the Blessed Mother. We noted how she was a mother to all of us; not just Catholics and Christians; but we were all her children.

We watched many of her apparitions from around the world, laughed and joked, and became very close friends. Life was wonderful. Week by week I became closer and closer to the Blessed Mother and Saint Theresa.

I began asking for more signs because I knew she sent me the medal. I also knew Saint Theresa showered us with roses so I asked the Blessed Mother and Saint Theresa to send me yellow roses as a sign that they were with me and they were hearing my prayers.

In order to rule out coincidence, I asked to receive a specific color; I needed to know 100%. It was an experiment. So began my open communication with the Blessed Mother through signs.

A few days after asking for the yellow roses I received a beautiful birthday card from my girlfriend Leona from the Bronx.

On the front of the card was a beautiful big yellow rose, surrounded with sparkles. Again, I got chills! But I still questioned whether or not this was real or just a coincidence.

Working with my friend Leona at 120 Wall St. N.Y.C.

I needed to see something tangible, not just by faith. I guess I take after my dad, a man with a scientific brain. But that's not gonna stop me from asking the Blessed Mother for all my heart desires.

My next heart's desire came immediately. I told Jimmy I wanted to start a family. He agreed. I told him at some point I would also like to adopt an oriental baby girl. Again he agreed.

My dreams were coming true. I wasn't sure if they came from up above but I was going to continue asking. There was no stopping me now.

Love proves itself by deeds, so how am I to show my love? Great deeds are forbidden me. The only way I can prove my love is by scattering flowers and these flowers are every little sacrifice, every glance

and word, and the doing of the least actions for love.

St. Therese of Lisieux (Little Flower)

A Rose by Any Other Name

Two years after the birth of my beautiful baby boy James, we decided to adopt that baby girl and have a sister for my James. I contacted a well-known orphanage called Mount Loretto.

It was only five minutes from my home, and the manicured grounds were park-like and so serene. Whenever driving by, I always had a wonderful feeling. When I called Mount Loretto I spoke with a woman named Dellis Carey. She told me that there was a very long waiting list to adopt a baby.

I told her that I prayed for an oriental baby girl for many years after I saw all these babies getting off the plane at Kennedy Airport. The adoptive parents were all there greeting their new babies. It left such an impression. I said, "One day that will be me!" Dellis said that the easiest route to adopt is through foster care.

So I agreed and we got licensed. I fostered many children in the first 2 years but no babies. Even so, I never lost faith that one day it would happen; I'd get that phone call.

I continued to go to the Miraculous Medal Novena and had the Rosary at my home. We started with four other women and me and soon ended up with about 15 people weekly. We all gathered in the living room where we recited the Rosary by candlelight. I would put out three statues of the Blessed Mother.

They were Our Lady of Fatima, Our Lady of Garabandal, and Our Lady of Guadalupe. These are three of many cities in which the Blessed Mother appeared. Each week, we dedicated ten Hail Marys to people in need. The girls always dedicated the last decade of the Rosary to me.

We would pray for a happy, healthy baby girl named

Christina because it was my mom's name, and Jimmy and I really wanted a sister for James.

When the Rosary was over, we would gather around the dining room table to have dessert and coffee. We would often tell funny, clean, and naughty jokes. Although everyone had that spiritual side to them, we were also grounded and down to earth.

We also spoke about the Blessed Mother's apparitions and watched them on videos. One of our favorite videos was the apparitions involving Conchita Gonzalez. The Blessed Mother and Saint Michael appeared to her from 1961 through 1965.

These videos made me feel I was a part of the miracles and a real child of the blessed mother. She was truly alive for me, larger than life; our heavenly mother who comes to earth and tells us how much she loves us and protects us.

Watching the videos brought us closer to the Blessed Mother. Meanwhile, at that time I had a lot going on in my life. I juggled a family, a full-time job on Wall Street, and our friends through the police department.

On top of all that, now I started a Rosary group. Yet somehow this group filled me with such peace and joy that it gave me the strength to navigate the rest of my life.

Always pray from the heart, and know that I always hear your wants and needs.

Blessed Mother

Praying from My Heart
Every morning while traveling to work, I would pray to Blessed

Mother on the bus. She said in an apparition to the children that we should always pray from the heart, and know that she always hears our wants and needs. I prayed for my family and friends and I prayed that one day I would be able to adopt a happy, healthy baby girl I promised to name Christina Rose after my mom and her twin sister.

For over a decade, I was praying to adopt this happy healthy baby girl named Christina — and my prayers were still not answered. The Blessed Mother had always answered my prayers so quickly that I got spoiled. Even so, I trusted her long enough to know that if she was going to bless us with this miracle baby, it would be on her terms not mine.

My daily prayers to the Blessed Mother were to watch over my beautiful son James and reminding her that I would love to have a little sister for him just in case she forgot. I trusted her every word, "Pray from the heart and if it's out of love and meant for the greater good, your prayers will be answered."

Ok Mother here's my prayer from the heart. "Send me black roses; not the yellow ones this time. I need black roses in a special way; in a way that would awe me; not only to know that you're answering my prayers but to know that my heavenly mother is really communicating with me. I don't see or hear you but I don't have to; these omens are my communication with you. Amen"

One day while at work, I received a phone call from one of my Jewish girlfriends, Janet. She said she just came back from visiting the Vatican and she bought me a gift. What an odd and intriguing call; my Jewish friend went to the Vatican, and she has a gift, from the Vatican, for me.

That night she came over to my home with a beautiful pink box that had a shimmering red flower on top. When I open the box, I was flabbergasted at what I saw. It was a beautiful silver filigree brooch, and in the center of this brooch was a hand-painted black rose!

I couldn't believe my eyes. Also, I couldn't believe my ears when

Janet told me she had it blessed by a Cardinal in St. Peter's Square. I was speechless. The Blessed Mother sent me a black rose in a way that truly amazed me. This sign was definitely impactful and certainly, one I have always remembered. Good one Blessed Mother, I feel so hopeful now that I will receive a call from Mount Loretto saying, "We have your baby girl!"

I felt astonished, but Janet looked at my face and asked why I looked so puzzled. I told her I prayed for a black rose on the way to work, just this morning. We both started to laugh and Janet said it took your Jewish girlfriend to go to the Vatican to answer your prayers.

Just when I thought that getting this black rose was enough of a prayer answered, the Blessed Mother had more events in store for me. The following night I was having dinner at my parent's home when I noticed a black object in my mother's China closet. It was more black roses! I couldn't believe it.

My mother just got them as a party favor two days prior. Again I got goosebumps and felt excited. My mother gave me the roses and told me never to forget how lucky and blessed I am. I was on a mission! I knew she was around me; that was for certain. I know my prayers were going to be answered.

Pray from the heart like a child would speak to its mother

Blessed Mother

Let us run to Mary, and, as her little children, cast ourselves into her arms with perfect confidence.

Saint Francis de Sales

Rita's Story

One evening, I was in bed reading, *Medjugorje: The Message* by Wayne Weible, one of my favorite books. He was a protestant who went to Medjugori to find out why these six children were claiming they have visions of the Virgin Mary. Wayne was walking up the mountain near St. James church where the apparitions took place.

Along the way, Wayne found a postcard face-down on the ground. He picked up the card and it read "June 18th, 1986". He found it very strange since it was only May 1986.

While reading this book, Jimmy came home from his shift at 1 a.m. He was exhausted and collapsed in bed. He asked me to turn off the lights so he could sleep. I said, "Very soon", and he immediately started snoring. I, on the other hand, kept reading.

I began reading a chapter called, Rita's Story. Rita is Rita Klaus, a woman who was forced to leave the convent due to her ever-increasing paralysis and pain, and eventually requiring a wheelchair and walking braces.

At one point she received a dire diagnosis about her declining future health and mobility. Her pain was at a high mark. One night as she lay down to sleep, she heard a gentle voice say, "Why don't you pray for yourself?" She responded with a prayer, 'Blessed Mother, please ask your son to heal me in any way I need to be healed.'

The following morning she was attending a class when she began to notice a feeling in her legs, and throughout the class, she felt her legs getting stronger. When she arrived at home she got out of the car and walked to the house without her wheelchair.

Once inside, facing the staircase, she knew she was completely healed. She took off her leg braces and started walking upstairs. After a few hesitant steps, she became overjoyed and ran up the rest of the stairs.

Reading this, my heart was pounding. Could this really be true? Did this miracle really happen? Back to the story. When her husband and daughters came home and saw Rita dancing around, they too began dancing with excitement. Rita's symptoms never returned.

It was a miracle, and Rita decided to go to Medjugori to thank the Blessed Mother. While she was there, she met Wayne Weible. He asked Rita if she would share her story with him. She replied, "Wayne I will never forget that date, June 18, 1986."

He stopped her and told her about his first visit to Medjugori in May 1986 and found a postcard pre-dated June 18, 1986. They both realized there was a divine connection between the two of them. They hugged each other and cried.

I, on the other hand, got shouted at, "It's three o'clock in the morning!" My heart jumped a beat. I looked up. It was Jimmy who woke from sleep. He was livid. "Turn off the lights for God's-sake."

This story had me on edge; I was ecstatic. There was no way I was putting this book down now. Jimmy could sleep on the couch for all I cared.

Back to my story before I got so rudely interrupted. I finished Rita's story without interruption and put the book down. I was wowed. Rita's story changed my life forever.

Years later Rita's story was such a miracle that the Unsolved

Mysteries TV show made an episode about her.

I turned the lights out. Oh my God, holy Moses. What the heck did I just read? She was miraculously cured just by asking the Blessed Mother for healing. I truly believed Rita's story and I said to the Blessed Mother. "If you really did heal her then you find my bracelet tomorrow." It was a diamond tennis bracelet that was missing for years.

My front yard in the Poconos
'The apparition'

Faith works miracles

George Meredith

Prayer is powerful beyond limits when we turn to the Immaculata who is queen even of God's heart.

Saint Maximilian Kolbe

The Bracelet

Reading about Rita's miracle last night was a life-changing moment for me. And asking the Blessed Mother to find my bracelet - it all was something I will remember for the rest of my life.

Yet this morning when I awoke, I forgot all about it. I had to clean the house, bathe my son, and take him to school. I'm not a monk who has all the time in the world to think about the Divine.

That afternoon I drove my son James to preschool. I came home and walked into the kitchen and flipped on the light. I froze in disbelief. My heart was pounding out of my chest. There it was, glowing all alone on the granite countertop, in front of my beautiful plant window.

I felt jubilant. At that moment I heard Jimmy's footsteps upstairs and I began to scream like a lunatic. "Jimmy, where did you find my bracelet!?"

He said he was taking his police uniforms out of the washing machine and saw something shining at the bottom.

I said, "I can't believe it! I can't believe it. It's been missing for 8 years and last night I asked the Blessed Mother to find it for me. Look at it, it's sparkling and gleaming!"

Jimmy said, "Of course it is, it's been bleached for years what do you expect?"

I want to emphasize that while I was ecstatic about getting my beautiful bracelet back after all that time, I was even more elated that the Blessed Mother answered my prayer.

I immediately put the bracelet away for safekeeping — it was never, ever seen again. Although I was saddened that I never found my bracelet again, I felt even more grateful that I had developed unwavering faith.

There was no doubt about it. She gave me all the proof I needed. *Now I feel she really healed Rita and she answered me*, I thought. I had to let that sink in for a moment. This was big. OK, it sunk in. In that moment, I was thinking maybe the Blessed Mother was telling me, adoption may not be necessary - just have a baby.

Suddenly I saw Jimmy as he was getting ready to leave for work. He was his usual calm self as he prepared to walk out the door. "Not so fast", I said. Jimmy looked up from his calm demeanor. "Jimmy I got something to say. I want a baby now."

"Where the heck did this come from?

We were standing in the kitchen next to the counter with the bracelet still sitting there. I picked up the bracelet and said, "I asked the Blessed Mother to find this bracelet at 3 a.m. this morning. Now it's 12:30 in the afternoon, and here it is! No doubt about it. I repeat. No doubt about it! I'm going to have a happy healthy baby girl named Christina.

Jimmy's demeanor changed from calm to confused! "Now you really lost your mind. "Life does not that work that way.""

I told him, "Oh yes it does, you'll see."

Jimmy shook his head dumbfoundedly and left for work.

Shortly thereafter I found myself eating for two. As I rubbed my belly, I thanked the Blessed Mother for this happy healthy baby girl named Cristina.

Jimmy & Mary
1990 Nansen's Lodge
Police Picnic

Mary is our mother, the cause of our joy. Being a mother, I hav never had difficulty in talking with Mary and feeling close to her.

Saint Teresa of Calcutta
(Mother Teresa)

Guess Who's Coming To Dinner?

I was confident I was having a baby girl; a sister for my son —

very exciting! I went out and bought cute little dresses, bows, and frilly, lacy socks and booties. I was going to have the All-American family.

Meanwhile, our weekly Novena group grew large enough that we moved it to the church. I told my everyone that my prayers were answered, "I'm having a sister for my son." You know the old saying, *Be careful what you ask for*. Well here's my story.

It was Tuesday, Feb 9th, 1993, what should have been another average day. Instead, a series of events unfolded that made my head spin.

The day started off normally. I bundled my son up in his red winter jacket and NY Giants hat. We were walking out the front door when the phone rang. My 4-year old son said, "Mama, answer the phone." The way he said it, the expression in his eyes, made me feel a sense of urgency.

"I can't James, I gotta get you to school."

"Mama you gotta answer the phone." he sweetly said. I had no choice, I picked up the landline receiver.

"This is Dellis Carey. I'm calling from Mt. Loretto. I have a foster child that we need to place. Are you able to take her?"

I told her I wished I could help but I'm 3 months pregnant and I thought it would be too much for me. Dellis said she was sorry to hear I couldn't take her because there were no available homes at this time.

Oh, my heart sank when I heard that. I felt so bad. There was *no way* I was going to say no. I thought, *I'm taking her, even though Jimmy is working the day shift. He'll just have to find out when he gets home*. "Ok, bring her," I said.

Then I asked Dellis when she was coming. She said the agency will bring her to my home tomorrow night, "They will bring everything I needed. Just have sterilized bottles and newborn diapers." I hung up and got my son to school on time.

As I dropped James at school I told his teacher I'm getting a baby tomorrow. She asked what was the baby's name. I said I never even asked. When I got home I called Dellis back.

"Dellis I forgot to ask you, what was the baby's name?"
She said, "Oh, her name is Christina."

I felt faint. The blood rushed from my head. I fell into the chair dazed and confused.

Shocked, I said, "Dellis, but I'm having a girl and her name is Christina.

She replied, "Mary, you're probably having a boy and she's meant for you."

My head was spinning. I called my next-door neighbor Marie, aka 'Louise' to come to my house right away. She ran over immediately wondering what the emergency was. I told her we needed to buy bottles and diapers because I was having a baby girl coming to the house tomorrow night.

She looked at me shocked and puzzled and said, "What did Jimmy say?" We laughed hysterically when I told her I hadn't told him yet. She said, "Oh no, please tell me you didn't." "Ok, I won't tell you."

We ran out to CVS and brought diapers, bottles, and some cute onesies. I already had the clothes, socks, booties, and pacifiers. After all, I was carrying a girl. [repeated above]

When we got home, Louise and I were sterilizing the bottles in my kitchen when guess who came home. I baffled him again. "What the heck are you girls doing?"

"We're sterilizing bottles, what does it look like we're doing" I blurted out, full of emotion."

He said, Why are you doing that now? You got 7 months to sterilize bottles."

I excitedly said, "We have a baby coming tomorrow."

"Whose having a baby?"

"We are."

"What the heck are you talking about?"

Louise interrupted, "I think this is my cue to go home." "You're not going anywhere,"

I commanded, "You stay right here; we got bottles to do."

Turning back to my husband I explained, "Jimmy, I got a call today. We have a baby girl coming tomorrow night."

Oddly, Jimmy asked, "What is her name?"

I replied, emphasizing her name slowly and clearly, "Chris-ti-na.

Jimmy and Louise both screamed at the same time, "Are you kidding me?"

All three of us were baffled.

Louise and I went back to the bottles, laughing and wondering if this really was the work of the Blessed Mother. I was pleased to see how gracious Jimmy was about this whole situation.

That night while lying in bed trying to make sense of all this I asked the Blessed Mother, "What the heck is going on here? Why are you giving me two Christinas? I'm really confused. Or maybe Dellis was right and you're blessing me with a boy *and* a girl? James may end up with a brother and a sister."

Maybe that's why he compelled me to answer the phone. Kids can be really intuitive. Sometimes they can really surprise us. I asked the Blessed Mother for answers and all I heard was Jimmy's nightly snoring.

The next day was another whirlwind. Louise and I shopped for cold cuts; capocollo, salami, mortadella, prosciutto, Italian bread, and cannolis; it cost me a fortune. It was a feast.

My neighbors came over, and so did my in-laws. We were all hungry but waited for the agency to show up. Then we could ask questions while we all feasted.

At 6 p.m. the doorbell rang. I opened the door and a gentleman entered carrying baby Christina in an infant seat. He placed her on the floor, handed us the paperwork, told us to call the agency if we had any questions, and said good night.

I told him we set up a whole spread for him and asked him to please stay and have dinner with us. He said he had another baby waiting in the cab to be delivered. And promptly left.

We all looked at each other in disbelief. Jimmy pointed his finger at me, "She is never leaving this house." Look at that.

He was already a poppa bear. He was protecting his baby cub even before he laid eyes on her. I felt so proud of him.

Jimmy and I walked over to the infant seat to look at her. We could not believe our eyes. I said, "Wow, she looks oriental." This was just too much.

Christina Rose
Living proof miracles do come true.

The events of the past two days began to sink in. The phone call came out of the blue, James insisted I answer the call, a stranger just dropped off the baby and left, her name was Christina, and she was oriental! This was just crazy.

From the dining room table, I heard my father-in-law shout, "Hey are we gonna eat or what?"

For eight years I prayed for this baby and I got everything I asked for. I felt so blessed. As Jesus said, "Ask and you shall receive, knock and it shall be opened.' Well, I opened the door...

Happy healthy, baby girl, Christina Rose, welcome home!

Some people say the stork brings our babies. In my case, I

really know who brought my child.

Daddy's little girl; protected from Day-1

Johnny at 1-year old

*Where the heart is,
there is happiness*

Persian Saying

When Johnny Comes Marching Home

It was time for my 5-month checkup with my obstetrician. I was especially excited to get my first sonogram.

"Congratulations, you're having a boy" the doctor smiled.

"No doc, I'm having a girl!"

"That looks like a boy to me," he said.

I sat there shocked, but very happy. I'm having a baby brother for James and Christina.

My Johnny was born on August 5, 1993. He had a full head of

jet-black hair - he was beautiful.

Jimmy said, "Mary, there's nothing Irish about him." From his looks to his name Johnny Armando-Joseph was named after my father and grandfather. Interestingly, he was also the spitting image of my father and grandfather.

But what made him special was that he was so loving and gentle. All his peers, cousins, and friends would go to him for advice. Even his siblings went to him for guidance. He was an old soul.

Everybody loved Johnny. I would take him to visit my grandparents who got a real kick out of him. My grandmother

Nana Mary Salerno, was warm and funny. She loved to tell Johnny stories, and feed him.

Johnny with Nana Salerno

My grandfather, on the other hand, was a strict disciplinarian. Yet when it came to Johnny, he was the apple of my grandfather's eye. Grandpa became very protective of Johnny, making sure he ate and was well taken care of. The kids called him big pop. It amazed me how well he took Johnny. Who is this man? He never treated us like that.

We would take Johnny to see big pop, but when it was time to leave he told us, "Go home, leave him here." What could I say? I couldn't say no to my grandfather. He wouldn't have listened to me anyway. My husband's a tough New York City cop. He couldn't say no to my grandfather either.

Grandpa ruled with an iron fist. No matter how old we were, we always saw that fist. So it was so out of place to see this tough guy proudly wheeling Johnny in his stroller around the block. Johnny shared so much love with others that he turned a lion into a lamb.

Grandpa Salerno —
'The Iron Fist'? and Johnny

His sister Christina mothered him from birth; 'Johnny do this, Johnny do that'. And Johnny did whatever she asked. To this day they are so close, like twins. And to this day she still tells him what to do.

Tina telling Johnny what to do at age 2

One day I was in the store with Christina. She told me there is a lady outside giving away cats and she was taking one home.

I said, "Absolutely not!" We got home with a cat on her lap. But after a short time, she didn't want to take care of it, and said, "Johnny you take it!" He took it. He spoiled it. They were inseparable. Johnny gave him the best life possible.

I am so proud of my son Johnny. He is currently working as a home inspector with his dad. One day Johnny will be taking over the family business. He is licensed real estate agent for Century 21 Carioti, and loves graphic design.

Johnny has always been spiritual and has a lot of faith. He is truly a blessing in our lives.

Thank you Blessed Mother.

Johnny & Tina's
first Holy Communion

Relative Miracles

In trial or difficulty, I have recourse to Mother Mary, whose glance alone is enough to dissipate every fear.

Saint Therese of Lisieux

Nana & Grandpa Salerno

Nana Salerno

Nana was my grandmother on my father's side. She was so kind, funny, and thoughtful. Her family was her everything. Everyone went to her with their life stories. She always had an open ear to it all, and always had the best advice.

Her door was always open; people came and went as they pleased. Nana was like a saint to us all. She also was the best storyteller. I could listen to her for hours. My father, Uncle Tony, Aunt Mary, and Uncle Junior all had the same knack for storytelling. They excelled at expounding funny and interesting tales.

When I listen to them I realize that the apple does not fall far from the tree.

In the 1990's I had a vivid dream of my grandmother. In the dream, she told me she had a tumor on her ovary. I was so upset but she insisted that this tumor was benign and I needn't worry about it.

I remember the dream like it was yesterday, when I asked Nana, "Are you sure about this?" She said, "Absolutely. Please, honey, do not worry about me, I am fine."

When I awoke I said thank God it was just a dream. But two weeks later, my mother told me that Nanna's doctor found a tumor on her ovary. Needless to say, my family was very concerned. I called my grandmother to tell her about my dream and assured her everything would be all right. Nana said it was all in God's hands. The dream was so real; that I knew all would be well.

She went into surgery about a week later. Of course, her whole Italian family was there: my mother, father, Uncle Tony, Uncle Junior, Aunt Mary, Aunt Pat, my sister Janice, and more. On the other hand, I stayed home because I knew she was fine. Completely fine.

I received a phone call from my Aunt Mary saying the doctor is still in surgery and the family is very worried. It was not supposed to take this long.

I told her that Nana is *fine*! She screamed at me. "How can you say that? How would you know that? I said, "Because I can *feel* it." My answer didn't go over big with her. If I told her I dreamt it, she would have thought I lost my mind.

Frustrated, she told me my father and uncles were pacing the floors, thinking the worst.

I told my aunt not to worry. I promised her that Nana would be totally fine. Get this, I'm telling my aunt who's strong as an ox what to do. Remember my grandfather with the iron fist? This woman is the daughter of the man with the iron fist; she's that tough. And I'm telling her what to do.

She abruptly said, "We'll see."

I said, "Yes we will."

My sister Janice called me with the results. She said the doctor had good news and bad news. The good news was that they successfully removed the tumor and it was benign. The bad news was my grandmother couldn't have children anymore. The family laughed feeling blessed and relieved

The Salerno Family

L to R: Uncle Tony, Aunt Mary, Nana Salerno, Grandpa Salerno, Dad, Uncle Jr.

Whatever you ask for in prayer, believe that you have received it, and it will be yours.

Jesus of Nazareth

Mama Mia

In December 2015 my mother was diagnosed with breast cancer. I worried if she was mentally strong enough to get through that frightening ordeal.

Along with my friends and family, we prayed very hard. I even had several rosaries said at my home with close friends such as Adicta, Anne, Mary, Jane, and Carol. Even my Jewish girlfriend Sybil participated in the prayers; the Blessed Mother says we're all God's children.

The Blessed Mother says prayers are very powerful, especially when we pray from our hearts. She clarifies that when we pray, talk to her like we talk with our mothers. So that's how I pray to her.

It was a very cold, icy winter in the Poconos. The doctors and hospital were approximately 45 minutes away. Driving to her appointments became extremely treacherous. It was one of the worst winters we had in a long time. We had ice storm after ice storm that never melted until well into the spring.

One time as we went to the hospital a car in front of us spun out. I thought for sure we were going to hit it. I prayed to the Blessed Mother, angels, and saints. Silently, I prayed over and over, "Surround this car with the Holy Spirit" Just then, that car miraculously spun out of our way and left an opening for us to drive through. Thank you. Wow, that was close.

Eventually, our prayers were answered; my mother's surgery was successful. Moreover, every time she went for treatment, she got stronger emotionally. She would optimistically say hello and smile at the doctors, nurses, and staff.

My mother looked beautiful in the stylish wigs that her dear friend Anne took her to buy. Not just one time but several times. Anne made her laugh and made the shopping for wigs a lot of fun. I saw strength in my mother that I never knew existed. She showed so much grace, fortitude, and courage throughout that tumultuous time. I knew she was getting back to her old self when she was worried about us again. She was putting us first. The focus was on her family. My mother was back! She did it! Together with the Blessed Mother, who never left her side, my mother conquered and persevered!

Nana Maria & Grandpa
Umberto Caligiuri

Lord, make me an instrument of thy peace... Let me sow love.

Saint Francis of Assisi

Maria Spina Caligiuri

No words can describe how kind and loving she was to everyone. For example, whenever workers came to the house, she would hug and kiss them all. She was that friendly; her heart was that big.

Both my grandmother and grandfather Umberto were born in Italy. Nana Caligiuri was an amazing cook and would tell everyone to *mangia*. I can still remember smelling her delicious homemade zeppolis.

We had an after-dinner ritual. Grandpa Umberto would bring out the guitar and Uncle Benny and Aunt Tina would start singing. How fortunate and grateful I am to have these wonderful memories. I had four loving grandmothers; two grandmothers, one great-grandmother Angelina, and Jimmy's grandmother Dinorah.

Then and now.

I also had two grandfathers, Umberto and Armando, who were extremely hard-working. Jimmy always said 'They could build a house out of mud'.

One thing they all had in common was their faith. They all loved Jesus and the Blessed Mother. There were statues all over their houses.

My grandmothers prayed in church with such devotion their faces shined with joy. Both my grandparents showed their faith through action. They loved and cared for their families as Jesus admonishes. All those images stayed with me.

My mother tells a story about the time her mother, Nana Maria, passed. On the day of her wake, my mother walked into the viewing and saw Nana in her casket wearing a beautiful pink dress.

But she was startled because she saw Nana sitting up in the casket. She said, "Mama, I miss you and I love you." My grandmother just stared at her with the biggest smile. To this day, telling this story makes my mother cry.

Great Grandmother Angelina Principato
(Nana Salerno's sweet mother from Italy)

Grandma Dinorah and Nana Salerno

Never stop dreaming and follow the omens.

Paul Coelho

Blue Jay Way

When Jimmy's youngest brother, Eddie, passed suddenly, I prayed to him for a sign, "Send us a Bluejay." The next day while gardening outside all day, many birds came, but no Blue Jays.

Pic by Richard Meehan

Later that night Jimmy and I were watching a movie on Netflix called *The Shack*. It was about a man who was having a near-death experience and was being shown heaven. The scene was celestial and the colors were heavenly; literally. While he was there a stunningly beautiful blue jay appeared.

"Oh my God, Jimmy, look there's the blue jay we asked Eddie for." I was expecting to see the bird in our garden, but he showed us in an unexpected manner. Just like in life he always did things his way. That made it even more special. Way to go, Eddie."

Love one another as I have loved you

Jesus of Nazareth

Pop Goes the Cardinal

Jimmy's father, 'Pop', passed in 2021. After the service, I told Jimmy to ask Pop to send us a red cardinal as a sign that he is still with us. That night when Jimmy came to bed I asked if he saw a cardinal. He thought he saw one, but it was getting dark out, and couldn't be sure.

The next morning, we went into the backyard to have our coffee, when suddenly we saw a big—very big—red cardinal. We never saw such a large one before. It was sitting on the bird feeder eating and chirping. I told Jimmy to look at how big that bird is. Your dad was a big man, why not send us a big bird? Pop did send us a sign. We love you Pop.

Worry ends when faith begins.

Unknown

Daughter Knows Best

One day my father went in for a routine physical and I called to find out how it went.

My mother said that the doctor saw a shadow on his bladder. I answered, "That doesn't mean it has to be bad."

My mother said next week they were going to do a biopsy. I told my mother to make sure she prays and I would too.

That day, while praying to the Blessed Mother, I pictured my father's bladder clear of any shadow. I thanked God and felt strongly there was nothing there!

The next day I repeated the process. But this time I wanted

to be certain my father was 100% well. I needed a sign to confirm this. I asked to be shown something yellow. Just then, my computer screen turned on by itself and displayed a bright, vibrant yellow background. Wow, that was odd, but I took it as confirmation!

Excitedly I called my mother and said, "Ma, I have to tell you don't worry about Daddy. His bladder's clear, there's nothing there."

"The doctor said they saw something," she shouted lividly. "Ma, I'm telling you there is nothing there," I repeated.

Frustrated, my mother said, "Okay that's enough, I don't

want to talk about it anymore. We said our goodbyes and hung up the phone.

The morning my father was going to get a biopsy on his bladder I called my mother to tell her not to worry.

I said, "There's nothing there." She replied, "We'll see". I kept telling her there is nothing there. She said she'll call me later.

While this biopsy was going on, I had 100% faith that there was nothing there.

A few hours later my mother called to say the doctor couldn't find the shadow. I emphatically said, "Ma, that's because there's *nothing* there!"

Not only was I so grateful and excited that my father got a clean bill of health, I was also excited that I was able to foresee this outcome. This was a serious health scare. Yet I had no worries —that's a miracle in itself. I felt such peace. How did I know? It's a knowing, I can't explain it any better.

This knowingness I just experienced gave me a deeper connection with the Blessed Mother. It strengthened my faith which brought me more and more peace.

I knew that the Blessed Mother was wrapping her arms around my mother and father and shielding them from harm like a loving mother would do. I was more grateful than ever.

Uncle Junior & my sister Janice

Give yourself up into the arms of your Heavenly Mother. She will take good care of your soul.

Saint Padre Pio

Touched by an Angel

Each member of our immediate family has various degrees of spiritual experiences. My mother gets signs all the time. My Aunt Rose sees her mother and father appear to her at night and also has beautiful visitation dreams from her husband. Aunt Mary was always sensing things before they happened. We all had various spiritual encounters.

Even my father who never spoke about spiritual things with the family had his own special moment. He was waiting in the hospital for hours while my mother was getting tests before her surgery. As my dad prayed he saw a penny on the hospital floor and immediately knew his prayers were answered. How did the penny answer his prayers? Because it says right over Lincoln's head, plain as day, "In God we trust."

The first person in our family to see an angel in the flesh was my sister Janice. One Sunday, she drove to Uncle Junior's and grandmother's house. Janice was going to stay with her while my uncle went to church.

Nana was 103 years old. Her bones were delicate. Sometimes she would get up and walk without paying attention. We were concerned she might fall and hurt herself.

Uncle Junior said goodbye to Janice as he drove away. When she got to the front door, Janice found it was locked. Panic set in. She checked all the doors and windows—locked. She ran across the street to a neighbor to see if she had a key—no key. The neighbor anxiously said, "Go get your uncle. I'll wait here and watch her through windows."

Janice flew in her car down to the church. The parking lot was packed and it took some time to find a spot. She rushed to the church, opened the door, and found it packed to the gills—standing room only. She was desperate now. "How am I ever going to find him?" As she scanned the crowd she saw a man walking toward her.

Without saying a word, he raised his arm and pointed across the room at Uncle Junior. Janice immediately rushed to her uncle. "I can't get in, your doors are locked!" Before she finished her sentence they were already out the door. They got in Uncle Junior's car and frantically sped back home.

Once they got inside they found Nana safe and still sleeping. They tried to calm down over a glass of Grandpa's homemade wine.

Janice said, "Thank God for that man!"

"Jan, what man," asked Uncle Junior.

"The man that pointed to you. I couldn't find you, the church was packed. Thank God that man showed me where you were."

"Jan I don't know any man."

"Uncle June, he looked right at you and pointed to you."

"Jan I don't know what you're talking about. I don't know anybody in the church. I'm home every day. No one knows me."

Janice said, "He wore a long overcoat, sunglasses, and a fedora on his head."

Uncle Junior thoughtfully replied, "Even if he was a friend of mine, how would he connect you with me? Jan, that doesn't make any sense."

"Then who was that man, and why did he point right at you?"

Janice had no explanation other than somebody was watching over them. This could be an episode of the TV show, *Touched by an Angel*.

My vocation is love

St. Therese of of Lisieux (Little Flower)

Anna from Grace

Some friends are based on sports, some friends are based on the job. I also had some friends based on prayer. There I was, making a hectic, chaotic commute to Wall Street every day with winds so strong that strangers had to hold on to one another; get up at 6 a.m. and walk through 3 feet of snow, rushing to catch our buses and trains to get to work.

And in the midst of all this madness, Marie, Anna, and I found a haven in Novena. We prayed for everyone who needed it and asked for our prayers. Praying and helping others took away our feeling of hopelessness. Do not tell me 'no.' Do not tell me there's nothing I can do. I've seen the impossible happen. I've seen miracles. That's how our special friendship was forged.

One day I got a call from Marie. She said Anna had something important to tell us and to come over that night. I heard the concern in her voice. That evening we sat in Anna's dining room with a cup of coffee in our hands and she began to talk.

Anna said she went to the doctors and just found out she was diagnosed with stage-4 ovarian cancer. Anna wanted to tell us personally. She also wanted us to know that she had decided to quit her job because she doesn't want to waste one more minute being away from her family. She also wants to spend more time with our family's close-knit Rosary group. My heart sank. I felt devastated inside while appearing calm on the outside.

She told us that she wanted to devote her life to prayer and to the Blessed Mother. Anna then looked at me and asked if I would mind allowing her to host the Rosary group at her home. Immediately I agreed. She was so grateful and said, "I love you girls. We, girls, are in this together to the end."

Over the next two to three years Anna showed so much grace through this. She was the consummate hostess. She tirelessly and happily hosted the

Rosary, serving coffee and cake; walking down 5-6 steps to greet each guest; that was a big deal. Anna did all this with a smile on her face. That's Anna in a nutshell.

Marie said to me, "Look how she's bringing all of us together for the Rosary. Look at all the people coming to her house. Wouldn't it be wonderful if we could do something special for her?"

We did.

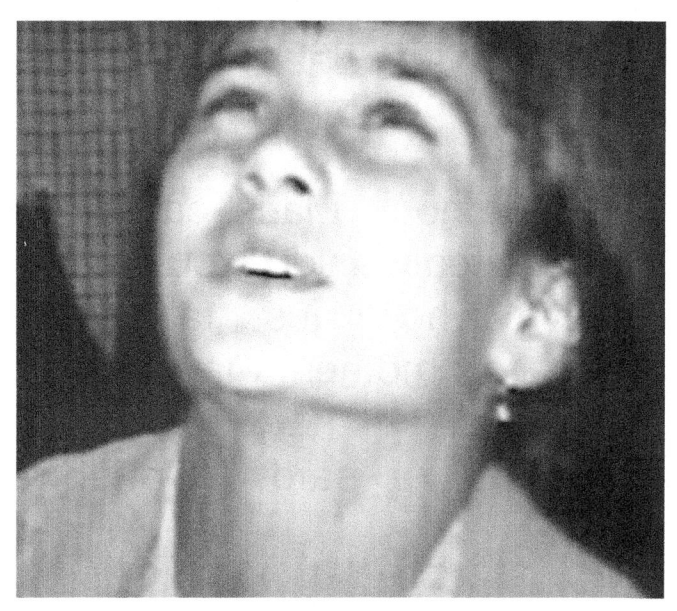

With God all things are possible

Luke: 1:37

Conchita Who?
I loved reading about people's apparitions of the Blessed Mother. I never imagined I would

actually get to meet one of them, but it happened.

One afternoon Marie called me and excitedly said, "You'll never believe who I just talked to; Conchita's mother-in-law."

Confused, I said, "Conchita who?"

Marie was talking about Conchita Gonzalez, one of the children who had apparitions of the Blessed Mother in Garabandal Spain. Marie read an article that said Conchita now lived in the United States with her husband.

She scoured the telephone directory for everyone who had her married last name and called them. Finally, one woman said she is Conchita's mother-in-law. By now my emotions moved from disbelief to excitement. Is she really this close to me? This is extraordinary.

Marie told her about Anna's serious health issues and asked if there was any way she could bring Anna to meet Conchita. Her mother-in-law said Conchita was overwhelmed by the wishes of her followers but she would ask Conchita to pray for Anna. She took Marie's phone number in case Conchita wanted to call her.

I was beside myself with joy. How special to have Conchita to pray for Anna. I wanted Marie and I to go see Anna and tell her.

This is the best news ever. But before we talked with Anna, the best news got even better.

As we were getting ready to call Anna, Marie got another phone call from Conchita's mother-in-law. We couldn't even have imagined; she said Conchita invited us to say the Rosary with her and her private prayer group. What a blessing. Now we really had something to tell Anna.

Marie broke the extraordinary news to Anna. We expected her to cry with joy; instead, she began to laugh boisterously. Between belly laughs Anna shouted, "Oh my God, you guys did that for me?!" Her infectious laugh quickly had us all belly-laughing.

We were so excited during the days leading up to meeting Conchita. At our Rosary group, we shared the news. That may have not been such a great idea. The day we left Anna's house to meet Conchita, there was a line of cars filled with members of our group who invited themselves to join us.

As we entered the church I was elated. It was really happening. I was about to meet this beautiful soul who was the closest person to the Blessed Mother in my lifetime. What did I do to receive this blessing? Then I saw her.

She was walking toward us smiling and holding out her arms to welcome us. It was heavenly. I was in awe. At that moment I felt totally connected to the Blessed Mother and Conchita.

Conchita graciously gave us the front pews and she and her parishioners sat behind us. It was exceptionally gracious because while she was just expecting Anna, Marie, and me, we showed up with an extra 15 people or so.

We all began reciting the Rosary. Suddenly I began hearing someone behind me reciting in Spanish (the rest of us were speaking in English). I turned to see who it was. I was delightfully surprised that it was Conchita sitting behind me!

It was so special to hear her recite the Rosary. While I listened to her, I felt mesmerized. I just wanted to listen, and absorb her angelic voice. In that moment I was feeling a spiritual healing of peace taking place for Anna.

I felt like it was yesterday. Here I was, an ordinary housewife, sitting next to Conchita who is praying for my friend Anna. It was surreal and very special. This was a moment I will always remember.

After the Rosary, Conchita handed Anna a beautiful blessed Miraculous Medal. Then she told Marie and me that she had something for us. Conchita brought out two rolled-up posters and said they were the last ones she had and wanted us to have them. It was so unexpected and appreciated. We all thanked her for this wonderful experience and said we will never forget her.

While leaving the church we unrolled one of the posters. I felt surprised to see a beautiful full-length image of Our Lady of Guadalupe. The following morning Marie went to the mall and had the pictures framed. They turned out so beautiful.

I asked Marie why Conchita would give us a poster of the Guadalupe apparition when her siting was in Garabandal. Marie had a philosophical answer. She said,

"There's a reason for everything".

We thought this was the end of the story. But about a week later, the story became even more miraculous.

Soon after, I went to visit my sister and found her with my parents sitting at the kitchen table. My father stood up and said he'll be right back. Janice asked where he was going. He said he was going to the Alba House bookstore to look for a full-length picture of Our Lady of Guadalupe.

Excitedly I told him I had one, and he looked very surprised. My dad said he had been looking all over for the full-length version. I immediately drove home and brought the picture back to him. My father looked at it and said, "Wow! Unbelievable."

For the last 30 years that poster has been hanging on my parent's wall. My mother and father wake up to that picture every morning.

I touch that picture every time I walk into their room. Even today, I am still in awe over the circumstances in which this poster was given to me. I'm so grateful for the special time I shared with Conchita.

Poster Conchita gave Mary &
now hangs on her mother & father's wall

When life gets too hard to stand, we kneel.

Unknown

Saved by an Angel

This story may seem out of place with the rest of the book. It is a story with a tragedy. But that's not the story. The story is about how an extraordinary event

126

changed my life. I know, all these stories were extraordinary and transformational, but this one — this one — is in a class by itself.

In October 1998 we welcomed our foster daughter, Sylena, right from the hospital at 5 days old. We called her Lena Ween — our whole family was taken with her.

My sons and daughter loved playing with her, making noises and flashing lights to see her light up with joy. Our kids loved playing with my dear friend Laura's children Jonathan, Nicole, and Dianne. We were one happy bunch.

This baby was too good to be true; Sylena always smiled and laughed. Whenever Jimmy and I went shopping with her we couldn't get out of the store.

Everyone stopped and stared and made a fuss over her — what a beautiful baby! She was so loved.
At one point I began to see signs of possible abuse from the biological parents. And despite all my attempts to protect her life, I was not able to save her.

This was an extremely difficult ordeal. We were the baby's parents in every sense of the word. We raised her, loved her, and bonded with her from birth. Please note, I'm intentionally skimming over this tragedy because I'm unable to relive it.

I said a special prayer. "Blessed Mother, once again, I look to you. It's you I come to. What's more, I don't even know what to ask for. How can I go on? I need to be strong; my children need me."

Desperately I prayed to her for help, and one night I was heard. After a particularly distraught night, I awoke and said to my husband, "Jimmy. I got to see the baby. The Blessed Mother put her in my arms. She was wearing a blue dress with pink flowers, white lacy socks, and white shoes.

You gotta believe me. It was so real, I remember every detail. Do you believe me?" For the first time, Jimmy saw a glimmer of life back in my eyes and said, "Yes of course I believe you."

Several years later I learned that dreaming about the Blessed Mother holding my heavenly baby was called a *Visitation Dream*. Mother, I also learned that it was you who put her in my arms.

The thought of that was exhilarating. What people would give for just 5 more minutes, and I got it. I will feel that forever. I am truly grateful to the Blessed Mother for this moment holding my beautiful Leena Ween. It truly was a life-altering experience for me.

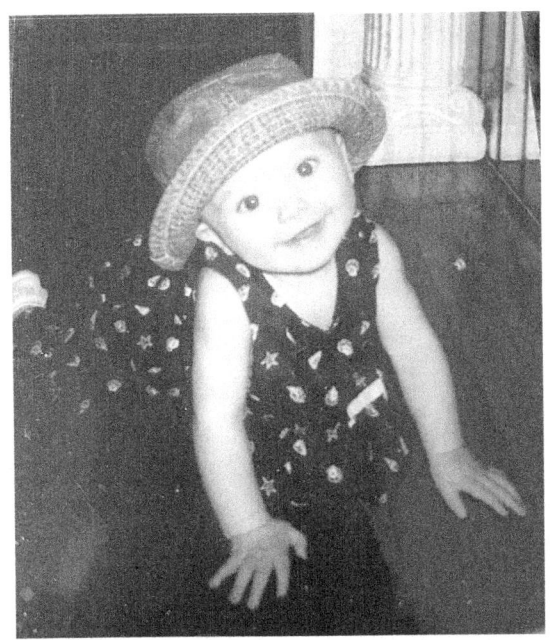

Sylena (10 months old)

My children (L to R) Johnny, James, Leena Ween, Christina

The Blessed Mother didn't lead me...to leave me

Mary Salerno Meehan

Life After Life

After an accident, my beautiful son James got his wings. This is another story of omission; I won't dwell on it because he's still here with me. When I ask him to show himself he gives me continual signs that he hears me. He was my son then, he's my son now, he'll always be my son.

The night before my son James got his wings was one of his happiest days for so many reasons. He had already passed his exam to work for the MTA. He was 'stoked' he made the list. Then he went to New York City with Jimmy to finalize his employment.

On the way, they stopped for lunch. James loved food, especially New York City Italian food. Of course, they stopped at the pizzeria to get his favorite, chicken roll. While the chicken roll was being made, the pizza smelled so good they had to have a slice. After lunch, they visited his Aunt Janice. James got to spend time with her and his cousins Keri and Kaila. It was a very nice visit.

Then James met up with friends he hadn't seen for a while. They went to a sports bar to watch the Mets and Yankee night games airing from the West Coast. This was one of James' happiest days. Thinking of it brings me comfort.

The next day Father John came to see me after James got his wings. I told him everything I felt; my grief, anger, confusion. He just listened. When I was done he said to me, "Just pray to him. That veil is very thin. He hears everything. When I lost my sister I asked her for a sign and I got it."

That meant everything to me. I told Father that makes sense. I pray to St. Anthony every time I lose something (where's my glasses, where's my cell phone, where's the remote). I keep St. Anthony very busy.

I pray to St. Theresa to shower me with roses; I pray to St. Francis to protect my pets. And I pray to the Blessed Mother above all. They're all humans. How is my son any different?

He said, 'Mary he is not different. Ask James for signs and you will receive them; just like I received them from my sister.'

I am so grateful for Father John. He validated there's life after life; James is alive. Heaven is eternal. I had to let that sink in. What's more powerful than this?

He also validated that we pray to the saints who are human, so I can pray to James. Thank you, Father John, it's an honor that you are part of our family. There are over 10,000 saints we pray to in the Catholic church — of course, we pray to humans. I am so fortunate to be raised Catholic. It helped me get to where I am today.

What a beautiful, powerful validation of life after life. I can speak and pray to my son and loved ones whenever I please. That is huge. Better still, they answer my prayers! That's validation in itself. Life has come full circle.

I grew up with the Blessed Mother, praying to her in the old world stone grotto at grammar school. We would crown her in the month of May, singing beautiful hymns like *Immaculate Mary* and *Salve Regina*. I spent many lunch hours in the convent with the sisters, praying in the chapel, while my classmates were at recess. Sister Cornelia asked why I spent so much time in the grotto. I asked her if it was OK for me to always be praying to the Blessed Mother. She said that Jesus says, "Anyone who honors his mother honors him and he can see the love in our heart."

Mary, Sister Cornelia, Cousin Frankie

I also enjoyed cooking with the sisters in the convent. These are some of my wonderful memories and the beginnings of my unshakable faith.

Two decades later, I met Marie on the bus. She invited me to a Blessed Mother Novena that brought back all the warm memories from praying to her as a child.

Now the Blessed Mother showed me that there is life after life, and Father John confirmed it. That is what is helping me move forward to make new memories with my James and Leena Ween.

"The way I see it, if you want the rainbow, you gotta put up with the rain."

Dolly Parton

Rainbows and Rain

In my life, whenever it rains, the Blessed Mother also brings rainbows that comfort and strengthen me. That was true in this case. The month after James got his wings my beautiful daughter Christina got married.

Christina at home before the wedding

There was such grace, miracles, and blessings occurring. I feel it was all orchestrated by the Blessed Mother — after all, Tina was brought out of the blue and handed to me at my front door.

And this baby girl grew up to marry a wonderful man, Steven, who is kind, respectful, and has a lot of patience. He's a hard-working man, and on his days off he helps the whole family. He's another son to me.

Another blessing is his mom Denise, like me, is a New York Italian, and Tina just adores her — two peas in a pod — my daughter loves and respects her Mama 'D'; partners in crime, LOL.

In one hand I held the storm, and in the other, I held a rainbow. It was the rainbow that pushed me through the storm; you gotta go through the storm to get to the other side. The rain subsided on the day of the wedding.

Christina's Wedding Day

This was a big event. Alphonso and Aunt Rose came from FL; Ann, Ed, and Melinda came from NY and NJ; and Steve's relatives came from all over. The wedding was held at the Raddison in Scranton, PA for about 200 people. I put this wedding together with my BFF friend Adicta and Mama D.

My BFF Adicta

"How were you able to put this event together after last month?" This is the question everyone asked.

I said I believed there is life after life. I prayed every day to the Blessed Mother to help me find my beautiful boy. And I prayed to my son every day. "I promise I will find you! No matter where you are I will find you!"

I was going to regain our spiritual connection — a bond between mother and son can never be broken.

Salerno/Meehan Family Photo

Meehan Family's Photo, June 2018
The last picture taken with everyone together.

Summary

Over the course of my life, I have been blessed to realize that life doesn't end here on earth. The Blessed Mother, Jesus, the angels, and the saints brought me miracles and signs that validated my belief that there is life after life and gave me the strength and courage to move on.

Because I know this is not the end when it comes to my loved ones, it's been easier to figure out how to navigate this life. Over these years, I learned many lessons on how to handle my grief. In the second part of this book, I will share some of the lessons that have been a big help for me.

Part Two

Discovering the Grace of Peace: Lessons I Learned

There were many places I found answers to heal; firstly from the Blessed Mother, and also from the tangible omens I received. [Some people believe the word 'omen' is a dark word because they saw the movie *The Omen*. It just means a sign from God.]

These harbingers profoundly affected me because they were non-disputable, concrete experiences. I expected to see big signs because I got them in the past, like when my daughter Tina was delivered to me in my home.

In this section I am sharing with you the lessons I learned that helped me overcome my grief. I hope they can help bring ease to your life too.

Receiving Signs

The magic in this world seems to work in whispers and small kindness

Charles de Lint

Penny for Your Thoughts

The first life-changing sign for overcoming grief I received was on Sept 20th, 2018. It was 3 a.m. and I was sitting alone at my kitchen island. I was in deep thought praying to my beautiful boy, James. I told him that he had to send me a sign. It had to be specific.

I said, "I want you to send me yellow roses. But you love red ones. So send me red roses instead, but they have to be special so I know it's from you."

With that, I went upstairs to lie down. Sometime after sunrise, Jimmy woke me up. He was baffled and said, "I just opened the door to let the dog out and I heard something drop. When I looked down I saw a penny." Jimmy had no pockets in his clothes; he wondered where the penny came from.

He said our daughter Tina was with him. She told him to look at the date. They were shocked to see the printed date, '1988'. He said, "That was the year James was born. And today is my birthday. I know James sent me the penny to say happy birthday."

I was in what is termed, 'a grief fog' and unaware it was even Jimmy's birthday. I told Jimmy, "I'm so happy that James sent you the penny." Then I said to James, "Thank you for doing that; that was so beautiful. You don't have to send me roses anymore."

That evening after dinner, Jimmy and I decided to watch a movie. We had to be selective about what we saw so we weren't triggered by sad stories.

Around midnight we were still watching movies when my son Johnny walked in the door from work, "Ma, I bought you roses tonight." I was stunned!

He said, "They had all kinds of colors but I bought you red ones." I was speechless. Johnny continued, "Ma, these are special handmade roses. You have to be careful, they are delicate. I told him how beautiful they were and how much I loved them.

Jimmy said, "This morning James wowed with me a birthday gift and now tonight he wowed you with the red roses. You got a beautiful gift from both your sons." And what a gift it was. I realized I still have my two beautiful boys with me. Their sweet love helped invite me back into life with my family.

James and Johnny…thank you
My heroes.

Faith tells me that no matter what lies ahead of me, God is already there.

Unknown

Another Penny For Your Thoughts

It was approximately 2 months since James got his wings when I received a phone call from my friend and neighbor Shirley. She asked me if I would be able to work one day fixing up an old traditional quaint cottage.

I didn't think I was up to it. But believing she really needed my help, I agreed. Later I learned she was just trying to get me out of the house that I hibernated in for three months.

I began working in the lovely cottage with this sweet Italian woman named Rosie. She started in one bedroom while I was close by in the next. We spoke about James, and I told her that somehow, someway I will find him. I continued to share all the beautiful blessings I have had from the Blessed Mother. Rosie was so compassionate, and I felt so comfortable speaking with her.

Then I shared with her about the penny that my husband Jimmy received on his birthday. I told Rosie we were so excited that the penny read '1988', James's birth year. That's when I noticed a penny in the opposite corner of the room I was fixing up.

While continuing to work I kept looking at that penny on the floor. I told Rosie that if James was here with us right now, he would send me a penny that would read '1988'. She was silent. I picked up the penny, it was worn out, and I was unable to read the date, so I just put it in my pocket and continued working.

A few hours later Shirley came to the cottage to pick us up. I told her how Rosie and I had a heartwarming conversation about James and all my blessings from the Blessed Mother, Jesus, angels, and saints. That's when we remembered the penny in my pocket.

Rosie asked Shirley if she can try and read the date on it. Unable to read it, she added my glasses and another pair that was sitting on the table. After looking at it with three pairs on, she screamed, "Oh my God, it's 1988!"

The three of us looked at each other stunned. I said, this happens to me so often, but I still get amazed and shocked.

Some may think it was a coincidence, but we knew better. Wow Shirley you were just looking to get me out of bed but I don't think you could've foreseen the blessing and validation I received from my beautiful boy that day.

A couple of days later I had my parents over for dinner. I don't know why I felt compelled to ask my father what he thought about my penny story. I knew he had received a penny validation that was meaningful to him but we never spoke about the afterlife.

My father had a scientific mindset and worked in a lab for many years. He was, and still is, so intelligent and book-smart. I really value his opinion. He is a genius to me.

Finally, I had the courage to ask my father if he believed that the 1988 penny I asked James for was indeed a sign. He looked at me with those dark brown eyes and said, *"It doesn't matter what I believe, it matters what you believe. If it was real to you, that's all that matters. Do not overthink it. It's all in the timing."*

Wow, that was big coming from him.

There's a quote by Arthur C. Clarke that describes my dad:

Magic's just science that we don't understand yet.

James, Christina & Johnny at Disneyworld 1998

Thank you Mary Ann Connors Natale for this special gift

Before you go to sleep
Say a little prayer
Every day in every way, it's
getting better and better

John Lennon

Beautiful Boy

A few months after the penny story, I decided I would try and listen to music once again.

It was early on a Friday morning when I got up and sat at the kitchen island with my iPad. It contained thousands of tunes but that day I only wanted to hear upbeat, happy ones. Cautiously played songs from PitBull, Enrique Iglesias, Reggae music, and cheerful country tunes.

I deliberately tapped each individual song on the iPad so that there WOULD NOT be any chance that it would accidentally play the John Lennon song *Beautiful Boy*! This was a song that I ALWAYS sang to my son.

When James was young I would sing it to him directly, looking into his eyes. But when he was older I indirectly sang it to him; he would walk into the kitchen & I began to sing it.

I just didn't look at him but he always knew *Beautiful Boy* was his song. Funny thing, looking back, while I sang, he never told me to stop. He would simply go about his business.

I was playing the up-tempo songs throughout that entire entire day & into the evening. But at 8 pm I was becoming weary and worn out. After a long day of diligently playing music, I finally shut it down & loudly yelled out, *"James where are you?* I cant see you but I will find you!"

Just then Jimmy walked into the living room & turned on a movie. Then out of nowhere, we heard a Japanese melody playing from the T.V. Instantly we recognized it was the John Lennon song *Beautiful Boy.*

Immediately Jimmy turned his head to look at me with shockingly, wide eyes and asked, *"Is that a sign"? "Is that a sign"?*

Shaking, I said, *"I don't know!"*

After a whole day of preventing the song from playing accidentally, as soon as I shut down the iPad, it played loud & clear from the television. What else was there to do other than shake my head, smile, and start singing to my beautiful boy.

Faith works through Love
Galatians 5:6

Traces of Love

Now that my angel babies are in heaven I also wanted to create a heaven on earth for us at home. I created sacred spaces to display their memories in our living room that included James' urn and Leena Ween's pictures.

Also, I incorporated life and all around them; Beta fish, live plants, a clock, and battery-operated candles that flickered 24/7. Giving life and light to my son and foster daughter brought me peace.

James' sacred space

Bringing life to James' memorial

In addition to this sanctuary, the Blessed Mother has graced me with hearing James telepathically and understanding Leena Ween's communication through feelings.

These experiences have opened up my 'realist' eyes to see a larger spiritual world. This has helped me develop new and divine memories with my heavenly family.

Tools I Use

As I walked down this path of healing it was a very lonely & scary journey. There were unknown feelings that surfaced around each bend in the road, and no end in sight. When challenges seemed insurmountable, I prayed to the Blessed Mother. Each time she showed me how to face and overcome the challenges. Over time they became tools that I could come back to when things got tough.

Below I've shared some of the the tools that have helped me the most.

- There is a marvelous organization, Helping Parents Heal, that works with angel moms, dads, siblings, and family members. They invite well-known theologists, authors, Near Death Experience (NDE), and spiritual speakers who help parents realize there is *Life to Afterlife*. (the title of their book).

There was nothing more important to me! The leading team, Elizabeth, Irene, Kathy, and several others were instrumental in helping me discover how to move forward and make new memories.

There are techniques that I use that help me get through the holidays, anniversaries, and other family get-togethers. At dinnertime, I always ask my loved ones to join us in an empty or imaginary chair so we are always gathered together.

- Another idea is journaling. I write down every sign I receive, big or small, so I'll always remember them. I also put photographs of signs I see in the journal. When I get into that 'rabbit hole' I open my journal. This helps renew me.

- For three years I didn't celebrate Christmas. Finally, my cousin Miriam said, "When James was a baby you nicknamed him Moose; Let's make a moose Christmas tree." I loved that idea. What a scene we created. Surprisingly, it brought me comfort and peace. Feeling James was with us while we decorated the tree made me feel he is a part of our Christmas.

James (Moose) loved sports

- One tip I shared with Helping Parents Heal was putting Jame's favorite snacks, Gatorade and Reeses, in his Christmas stocking. I could see him laughing when I told him, "Mama knows — I always remember to put your favorites in your stocking."

  Also, I ask my family and friends to write little loving notes to James wishing him a heavenly holiday. I leave the notes in the stocking and add to them every year.

- When I needed a sign from James, I asked him to send me a bluebird. As we are writing this Christmas story about James, for this book, a big, beautiful blue bird came from out of nowhere and landed on the bird feeder.

I never saw such a big beautiful blue bird before. I feel James sent me a sign he loves what we wrote. This is my wonderful divine life - this just happened in real-time. When I am open to communicating with my angel babies they answer — to this day — they let me know they heard me.

- One of the most important tools that have helped me through my journey was the love and support of my family and friends. In the first few months, I needed time for myself, away from everybody. I was unable to make decisions and couldn't handle any pressure.

But then I began to call my Uncle Junior and tell him how I felt nothing was real. I had no concept of time. This brilliant man always knew what to say and how to make me laugh. I am so grateful to have him in my life.

- Another tool is making a special donation in the name of a child. For us, the opportunity to use this tool came by way of our friends, Louie and Yvette Balestrieri.

They gave us a most heartwarming gift, a beautiful gold chalice engraved with James's name and birthday. What makes this gift so special is that the chalice is sacred in our church. So Jimmy and I were able to donate the chalice to Father John to use at mass for the Holy Eucharist.

Louie was Jimmy's partner in the Anti-Crime unit for the NYPD. Jimmy and I are grateful to Louie and Yvette for uplifting our hearts at that time.

The chalice

- A big thanks to my beautiful amazing sister Janice, and sister-in-law Margaret, as well as all my wonderful sister-in-laws and brother-in-laws. They all had a very special bond with James, and he loved them very much.

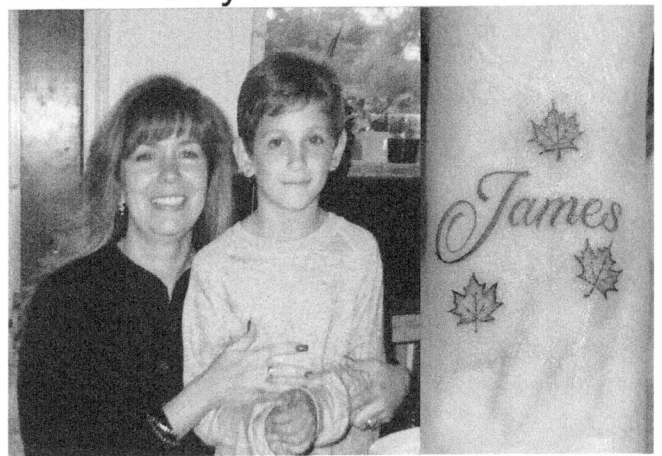

Margaret got a tattoo
to remember James

- There are other people I am also grateful for; my wonderful friends like Anne LeSchack who I am able to call for prayers and support anytime. Jesus said when two or more ask for the same thing, I will answer. Thank you for always being my second voice and for being a second mother to Christina Rose.

- My happy pill, Sybil immediately cracks me up before we even say hello.

My humorous friend Sybil and me with comedian Ralphie May

- Previously I used to spend time with my mother, helping in any way I could. During the years when my babies got their wings, I was not a good support for her or anyone. I am forever grateful to Anne, Helen, and my BFF, Adi for all the love they gave to my mother as my surrogate. They mean so much to me.

Also, a big thanks to all my family and friends that have walked alongside me down this lonely path. To name a few, Alphonso and Rosemary, Ricky and Kim, Gloria, Lisa and Marty, Liz and Gene., George and my beautiful nieces and nephews.

- Another major tool for me was faith. It was instrumental in helping to push me through the storm. I felt I was not alone. There was something or someone bigger than myself that I could trust. I read Corrie Ten Boom's book, *Tramp For the Lord*.

  Corrie had made all her decisions in life based on what she felt Jesus guided her to do. She had an incredible amount of faith. Much like Corrie, I felt secure surrendering to the divine, trusting that they were with me in my every move. I told the Blessed Mother, "You lead and I will happily follow."

- In the beginning of my journey through grief, I dwelled on the things that I should have done for my loved ones. This thought was like a knife piercing my heart. To help with pain, I began looking at their photos. Over time, the knife began to dull the memories helped ease the pain.

  This brought me solace; my eyes looking in their eyes and their eyes looking back at me. Three years of looking at all my pictures, I began feeling joy again.

L to R: Jimmy, Johnny, James, Al, and Tina 'On top of the world." at Universal Studios (1998)

The most precious, joyous times with our loved ones, I'm sharing here.

In the spring of 2000, we were living busy lives and Jimmy was working full-time for the police department. Yet we decided to open up an Ice Cream shop/

diner that we named, *Scoops Plus*.

Although it was hard work, our children couldn't have been happier. They were eager to work and help out at the store. They were just as eager to have all their friends come in and give away half the profits.

After school, my kids and their friends like Kaila, Jen, and Freddie would come and have their Philly cheesesteak, cheeseburgers, fries, and an ice cream flavor of their choice for dessert. It was a fun, happy environment.

Tina at Scoops

My father-in-law and me at Scoops

Our manager Linda Rago had a smile every day from ear to ear, and was such a pleasure to be around.

Linda Rago with my niece Kaila

After a couple of years of working every day without a day off, my Uncle Tony & Aunt Pat along with Linda insisted we take time off. Together with our kids & friends Ed, Anne, Melinda, Lucy, Jim & their kids, we drove 13 hrs to Myrtle Beach. We all stayed at a hotel on the beach. We also took my sons best friend Fredrick with us. Freddie and the kids said it was the best vacation they ever had. Sadly, Freddie got his angel wings approximately two years before James. We were all so heartbroken.

Frederick and James at Myrtle Beach
Forever flying high with the angels

James and Freddie were like brothers. He was so sweet and respectful. My son James and I felt so grateful that we were able to take him on this enjoyable 14-day vacation that he and the kids never forgot.

These memories are priceless. every time I question whether or not I did enough for my kids, this puts things into perspective.

Now I am able to look back on these wonderful amazing memories & thank the Blessed Mother for giving us a perfect fun filled 2-week vacation. For this I am very grateful.

At one point I heard the Blessed mother tell me, "Envelope yourself with your children." So I began blowing up their pictures and hanging them on the walls of my home.

Having these enlarged photos throughout the house made me feel our family members were continually with us, sharing our new memories. They were, and always will be a part of this family.

Miraculously, these photos and memories began bringing me glimpses of joy again. They showed me how happy my children were, and how much joy I was able to give them.

Enlarged photo of James

• My Essential Meditations

Humility & Grace

God gives grace to the humble.
James 4:6 NCV

Accept my teachings and learn from me, because I am gentle and humbler in spirit, and you will find rest for your lives
Matthew 11:29 NCV

The humble shall inherit the earth
Matthew 5:5

Gentleness, Patience

Gentle Father, thank you for helping me express more of your gentleness, patience, & tenderness,

and in my thoughts, words, and actions — no matter what comes my way.
Unknown

Generosity
God loves a cheerful giver
2 Corinthians 9:7 NLT

Faith
If you have faith the size of a mustard seed, you can move mountains. Nothing will be impossible for you
Matthew 17:20

Summary

My undermining feelings are never as bad as I first imagine

Mary Salerno Meehan

The miracles and foreshadowed events that I experienced restored my faith. They are what sets the foundation upon which I build my strength and courage to carry on.

As the saying goes, 'You have to go through the storm to get to the other side'. There are no shortcuts or any way around it. I had to face my losses and all the emotions that came with it. One moment I would feel angry. Then I would feel guilt, blame, and sadness. The guilt was the worst because it was so magnified in my thoughts. And blame; first I would blame God, then I would blame myself. My emotions were up and down like a wave. I never knew how I would feel from day to day.

Now I'm learning to ride that wave. I'm able to feel all the emotions knowing I'm facing them head-on even when it feels messy and hard. Over time, I've come to realize something that was a huge help to me; the undermining feelings that I had in my head were not as bad as I first imagined.

Now I embrace the courage and uncertainty because I know the Blessed Mother always walks beside me. I also know that Jesus gives me the grace to walk through that dark tunnel to the light of possibilities.

Epilogue

*Magic exists.
Who can doubt it, when there are rainbows and wildflowers th music of the wind and the silence of the stars.*

Nora Roberts

The Mount Carmel Medal

In June, 2023 as we were finalizing this book, I went to visit my parents & daughter in the Poconos.

My husband, son and I stayed at our original home that Jimmy and I had built and raised our children. Now Christina & our son-in-law, Steve live there.

I stayed in James' old room. I thought it would be difficult to sleep there, but instead I felt his presence comforting me.

For some reason, I kept speaking to my family about Conchita. I told them how grateful I was to have met her and how kind she was to us all.

On the morning we were leaving I decided to take one of my old vases home with me that I bought over 30 years ago.

I love monkeys and this vase has a monkey motif on it. As I went to pack it in my suitcase, I heard a clank. *"Oh,"* I thought, *"could this be a special penny?"*

The Monkey-motif vase

But as I turned over the vase, it wasn't a penny. A round 14 kt.

gold medal slid out onto James's mattresses.

The inscription read, *Our Lady of Mount Carmel*. It was so strange, no one in the family ever saw the medal before.

I searched online to learn about it. Magically, this medal was from Conchita Gonzalez's apparition in Garabandal, Spain.

I was shocked and amazed how this medal appeared on its own; out of the blue.

As I turned out the light, I smiled, thanking my beautiful boy for another wonderful sign, and left for the airport.

As this book goes to press, I look forward to a continued lifetime of new memories and magical surprises from James and all my loved ones.

Hail Holy Queen of Peace.

Our Lady of Guadalupe
Pray for us

About the Authors

Mary Salerno Meehan

Mary has contributed chapters in a few books including, *Beyond the Veil*; Angels Amongst Us. She loves interior decorating and cooking for family & friends.

Swami Sadashiva Tirtha is a #1 best-selling author, and has written several books on natural wellness, stress management, and spirituality. He loves playing guitar and spending time in nature.

Other Books by

 Peaceful Press

Available at amazon.com

Also available in Spanish, Turkish, Vietnamese

Made in the USA
Middletown, DE
29 July 2023

35586345R00126